Knife Island

Knife Island

TO: Don + Melinda

Love Tom + Marilyn

Circling a Year
in a Herring skiff

Stephen Dahl

ISBN: 978-1-932472-82-0
Library of Congress Control Number: 2009929435
Design and layout: John Toren

SECOND PRINTING

Photo credits:
Jason Bradley: 6, 55, 59, 68
Dave Brislance: 38
Stephen Dahl: 64
Douglas Fairchild: 2-3, 13, 48
Ann Jenkins: 15, 32-33, 43, 67
Cody Olson: 62
Shele' Tofte: 26, 50
John Toren: 30

Special thanks to Randy Ellestad for providing the historic photographs on pages 17, 18-19, 40, 41, 46, and 57

Nodin Press, LLC
530 North Third Street
Suite 120
Minneapolis, MN
55401

www.nodinpress.com

There are many gifts in life.
This book is dedicated to three very
significant gifts in my life.

James M. Dahl
December 13, 1924 – August 27, 2008

Barbara Rose Dahl

Georganne

ACKNOWLEDGEMENTS

Writing a story is a solitary act. But soon after it is finished, it unfurls like a field of flowers opening to the morning sun, to a wider community of friends.

A great big "Thank you" to the following friends and family that listened and helped "unfurl" this story along the way: My wife, Georganne; Louis and Ann Jenkins; Cree and Jason Bradley; Shele' and Harley Tofte; Gordy Olson, Kristi Kendall-Olson and Cody Olson; Jim and Pat Hanson; Stuart Sivertson; Mark Torgerson.

A "Thank you" to the photographers: Jason Bradley, who dealt with subzero temperatures; Douglas Fairchild, who was willing to bounce around in three and four foot seas; Ann Jenkins, Cody Olson, Shele' Tofte, John Toren and David Brislance.

"Thank you" to Randy Ellestad for the photos from his historical collection, and to Todd Lindahl for helping him put them on a CD; to Larry Rasmussen, who helped Orville Reese lift nets through the years; Dick Martin, who first told me the story of his grandfather, Magnus Martin; and to Jan Green, whose knowledge of the avian world is superlative.

I am deeply grateful to Norton Stillman for giving this book a chance and to John Toren for his meticulous editing.

Knife Island

PROLOGUE : Light southwest wind this morning. I steer northeasterly for my nets. A faint orange glow ahead. A few herring gulls pull off Knife Island to follow me as I go by, but soon lose interest. About a half mile from shore, near Stone Quarry Point, a streak of flat water. The gulls space themselves thirty yards apart along the edge of this colder surface water. A good scavenging technique.

My outside net is bowed into the sea. Southwest sea, northeast current. The net will twist as I slide it over the gunwales and pick herring. It's manageable today, but the twisting just makes it a little more difficult. If the current is quite strong and opposite the sea, I sometimes have to stand (or kneel depending on how rough it is) six feet back from the bow to spread the net. A light wind and current from the same direction make lifting a net easier—much easier. Regardless of the direction of the current when I first start picking the net, it can change halfway through, or

Opposite page: Torg and his Dad

it might just stop. I've seen a net set four fathoms below the surface bowed northeast, but when brought to the surface it pulled to the south.

My other net is only 300 yards to the north. It's bowed to the southwest. Tomorrow might bring north wind and no current with clear cold water. Tomorrow might bring northeast wind and current with warmer dirty water.

There are seasonal times—the most notable being at the end of July, first of August—when the current is sometimes so strong you would think the Yukon River is suddenly flowing through. My guess is it's because the lake's surface water has warmed considerably. A strong wind pushes the warm surface water to the shore where it curls under and pushes the cold water out. Combine this with a strong high- or low-pressure system and the water starts to move even faster.

At the end of each net, I carry fluorescent orange polyform floats, 60 inches around. They were designed and made in Norway to handle the North Atlantic. They help hold the net up and make it easier for trollers to see them.

Last summer, first of August, only 3 or 4 inches of the top of these floats were showing. It takes an enormous force to pull them down that far. I whispered to the net—"Hold on, don't snap an anchor"—and headed home, leaving them behind. It would have been impossible for me to lift them. Later that day I took the binoculars to Larsmont Hill to see if they'd popped back up, knowing that if they hadn't I'd just get them the next day.

MARCH 24 : I'm sitting in the swing that I've hung from the overhang of my woodshed. The shed faces to the south and the mid-morning sun has just peeked around the top of a white spruce. It feels good on my face. I close my eyes to the brightness. When you want the wind to blow— it doesn't. The ice is just sitting out there. It's not heavy, not land fast, and it only stretches from Duluth to just past Knife Island, 18 miles. Two days of southwest would send it towards Canada, and then I could get a net set.

APRIL 2 : The ice is gone. It might be in the middle of the lake or maybe it is jammed up against the Canadian shore. In front of me, as I stand at the end of the marina channel—is blue water. To the east is Knife Island. The herring gulls are back and for the next four months, Knife Island is their place to give birth and raise their young. A place far enough from shore to be predator-free—no fox, fisher or marten. An island small, windswept and rugged enough to foil the human predatory developer too.

My problem is behind me in the marina channel. There are still 75 feet of ice, ten inches thick, in front of the boat landing. If I had skids, this wouldn't be a problem. It's a simple setup—a couple of rails with crossbeams spaced two feet apart. A winch at the top. Slide your skiff into the water. When you come back in, grab the cable and hook it to the bow and winch the skiff up. This is how most of the early Norwegian settlers fished. And there are still fishermen up the shore that operate this way. But skids are unattainable for me. You need to own land on the shore to

Carl Erickson's dock and skids, circa 1950

operate them, and I started fishing on Lake Superior twenty-two years ago without a family connection to the shoreline. I make do. And though ice can be a problem for me in early spring or late fall, at other time going out of a marina is advantageous. There are days when your nets are "liftable"—three, four, five-foot seas—but try launching a skiff off a skid that's not protected in a cove or by a peninsula with four-foot seas pounding the shore.

Last year at this time I had the same problem, so I trailered my skiff up to Two Harbors. The boat launch in Agate Bay always opens up earlier than the Knife River Marina. The run from Two Harbors to Knife River isn't too bad. But with an eighteen-foot open skiff, I still "watched the weather" before heading out.

This year, I think I'll wait a few more days. A low-pressure system is coming in and that usually means northeast. A couple of days of northeast will lift that ice and bust it.

APRIL 10 : It was a good northeaster last week. It blew for three days. The ice in front of the boat landing broke up on the second day.

I have two nets set. One is a half-mile southwest of the marina and three-eights of a mile out from shore—the same place Squeak and Kenny set for over sixty years. They were brothers, close in age. They started tending nets when they were eight years old. The net is in front of their old homestead. Kenny died two years ago. Squeak's joints give him too much trouble to get in a skiff and pick herring. But he wants me to use "the set."

I picked "Squeak's net" first. There was only six pounds of herring in it. I'm almost finished with this one. I'm not even going to make six pounds. This net is located a mile and a half from shore and three miles northeast of the marina. Each net is 300 feet long and 14 feet deep. Much of the time, I set my nets at 4 fathoms (24 feet). Twenty-four feet from the surface of the water to the top of the net. The nets don't fish in the daytime, the water is too clear. You catch herring at night, when they come up in the water to feed. In the spring, when the water temperature is colder on top, I usually have to set them deeper. I've got them at 8 fathoms. I could keep adjusting them to different depths, but my gut tells me there just isn't anything around. Last year, I caught 4,000 pounds in 3 weeks starting mid-April. That was on two nets, totaling 600 feet—and some of the time I had to tie the nets up because I couldn't handle all the fish. But it might be starvation for a little while this spring.

APRIL 19 : When a net is full of herring, very full, it will sometimes float to the top when you lift it. On such occasions the herring gulls are merciless. You can shoo, yell, wave your arms and they won't let up. They pull the gills of the herring out first, then the organs right behind the gills, and it makes it damn difficult to get the fish out of the net.

It's what they did to me this morning. The current was flowing parallel with the net, causing it to float up. I finally gave up trying to scare the birds away, dropped the net back in the water, and tried lifting it from the other end. It was harder to lift against the current, but the ploy worked. The net stayed submerged until I lifted it over the gunwale.

I'm headed in now. I have 700 pounds of herring in my skiff. I can see eight people waiting for me at the dock. Word has spread I've had "big lifts." Knife River was a commercial fishing town. Knife River still is a commercial fishing town. Later today folks will be making fish cake batter, canning and smoking herring, and probably having their first meal of the season of fresh herring. I'm tired and happy as I tie up to the dock and fill their coolers and boxes up with fresh herring.

APRIL 20 : I'm headed back in to the marina, just passing by Knife Island. Three pelicans are standing on the rocks at the far western end of the island. They're the first ones I've seen this year. They aren't common here. I think I'm fortunate if I even see a dozen during the season.

The herring gulls are passing by regularly with mouthfuls of dead grass from the mainland. Nest building. There's a light northeast wind and the sky is gray.

I tied one net up yesterday. With this much fish around, one net will be enough for me to handle. I caught 325 pounds this morning. It's wonderful that the herring stocks have recovered. It wasn't always this way.

The herring stocks had declined with the introduction of smelt and increased pollution. The most notable source of pollution on the North Shore was Reserve Mining Company in Silver Bay. The taconite processing plant dumped 47 tons of waste rock in water slurry into Lake Superior every minute for 25 years before a court order stopped it. The gray water and sedimentation it caused were shameful. Herring need clear cold water.

Smelt are an invasive species that were first reported in Lake Superior in 1946. When an invasive species enters a new ecosystem, their population usually explodes and is disruptive. The population explosion of this slender 7-to-9 inch fish was probably exacerbated in Lake Superior because the population of its likely predator, the lake trout, had been greatly reduced by sea lamprey. Biologists are hesitant to acknowledge the disruptive element of smelt on herring, but commercial fishermen see it differently. Smelt have teeth comparable to larger predators like lake trout, northern or walleye. When the smelt population was vast, they probably preyed heavily on herring fry. We may never know for sure if we're weighing the causes accurately, but the chronology is interesting. Starting in 1976, the smelt population collapsed and then stabilized at a much lower level; Reserve Mining stopped dumping waste rock slurry into the lake in 1980; and by the mid-

I rarely use the fish-scaler. About 95 percent of the time I make skinless fillets.

1980s, the herring population was healthy again.

As I turn into the marina channel, I say farewell to the pelicans. I know they'll be gone tomorrow morning.

APRIL 21 : Wind is howling. Sailboat rigging clanging. Boat covers flapping. Herring gulls play on the updraft off the beach. And the heavy pounding of sea.

My skiff—the only boat in the water—is riding the storm well on the lee side of the gas dock. Time to go have coffee at Lawrence and Ole's.

Lawrence and Ole are brothers. Their house is across the road from Kendall's Smoked Fish in Knife River.

Eighty-one years old, Lawrence is the young brother. He rebuilt the front porch on their house last summer. When I walk in the back door, I can smell fuel oil. My guess is he pulled apart the carburetor on the fuel oil stove to clean it. He's usually got a project going every time I stop by.

Ole had a stroke a few years ago. Life moves at a little slower pace for him now. He doesn't talk much. When he sees me, he sticks both hands up in the air as if to say, "I didn't do it." He grins a mostly toothless grin and shuffles off to get me a cup of coffee. I knew Squeak was here too, his truck is parked in the driveway. He asks, "Did you check your skiff already? Not Lake weather today."

"Yup, it's ridin' well." Ole hands me my cup of coffee. "Thank you sir!" He nods. My son's mother-in-law would faint if she drank out of this cup. The stained cup gives me a little smile. One never knows the direction of conversation at this table. There is always talk of commercial fishing. And everyone needs to grit their teeth about President Bush. He isn't popular around here.

One time Lawrence said he needed to get clothes washed which led to buying new pants which led to laughter 'cause they both keep shrinking as they get older and they have to keep buying shorter pants. I remember when I left that day...wondering if I would be able to accept my later years as gracefully.

I finally remember a question I've wanted to ask them. "Kenny once told me a story about two fishermen that both had nets off Knife Island. It was just when they were converting to gas boats. One fisherman still used oars and had a helper in the skiff. The other one had a new gas boat. A hard northwest hit, making it impossible for the rowers to make it back to shore. They just had to hang on to the

Peter Bugge, herring skiff, 1939

net. The helper asked why they didn't wave to the owner of the gas boat for a pull to shore. The fisherman mumbled something about not taking a herring from him even if he was starving. They hung on to the net all day and rowed in when the wind died down in the evening."

After I'd told the story, I asked Lawrence: "Do you know the names of those guys?" Lawrence thought a bit: "It could have been any one of those old sons-of-bitches."

MAY 5 : The northwest wind is just plain mean this morning. Coming straight off the north shore, it wants to rip the net out of my hands before I can even pick the herring off. It's one of those days where it would be much easier to have two people in the skiff—one just to hold onto the net while the other takes the fish out. But I've figured out a

Fishing Village, Knife River, 1907, gaffe-rigged fish boat on skids.

way to work the net alone in a strong northwest. I've found I can clamp the cork line with the back of my upper arms to my chest, which leaves my hands free. But it's still frustrating and the expletives start to fly. My wife keeps telling me the universe is not personal. Most of the time I agree with her—but not this morning! This damn wind is out to kill me! It doesn't care about anyone else in all of Northeastern Minnesota—it's just after me!

I start laughing. I've really lost my mind. Who or what am I swearing at? I'm reminded of a story Stuart Sivertson told me. It was on Isle Royale. August. He was helping his dad, Stanley. They were fishing McCormick's reef. The

winds were calm. They had very few fish. Strong currents had set in and twisted their nets. When they had everything straightened out, they noticed Nels, who was working his nets to the east of them shaking his fists in the air. Even though there was no wind, they felt they should go over and see if he needed any help. When they got near him, Stanley asked if everything was all right? Why was he shaking his fists in the air? "I was yelling at God to come down and fight like a man!"

MAY 15 : The last few days have been cool with light rain. As I pass by Knife Island, headed to my nets, I can see that the lichen clinging to the rocks has turned a brighter green with the recent moisture.

Yesterday, as I was quietly sliding along one of my nets, three Bonaparte gulls swam towards me. I suppose they were resting and replenishing themselves before heading farther north, maybe to Hudson's Bay. I'm envious of their destination—a place of silence and wind. I suppose you might hear the faint din of an airplane or transcontinental jet occasionally.

On a return trip from Norway, in late May, I was on one of those jets. The sky was clear as we crossed the lower part of Hudson's Bay. I only saw one small lead of open water. The rest was covered with ice.

I had gone to Norway to do research on a Norwegian stringed instrument called a langeleik (long-ah-like). I make folk harps in the winter months, when I'm not fishing, and I wanted to learn how to make these langeleiks. As is so typical of Norwegians, the instrument makers and musicians I talked to were very generous in sharing information about langeleiks.

This wasn't my first trip to Scandinavia. I went to school for a year in Denmark. A few years later, I returned to Norway to work on a farm in the far north. I often think about my time there. Lately, articles in the Duluth newspaper have brought back my thoughts of Scandinavia. The discussion has been about social democracy. It astounds me how little this form of government is understood in America. And I'm further puzzled by the fear from which the politics of the right—especially the "religious right"—operate. The Scandinavian nations strive to be egalitarian. They have essentially eliminated poverty. No one worries about health care—it's covered, from birth to death. Aren't these goals that the evangelical right would wish to pursue?

And then comes the usual "but socialism takes away the drive to work." But it isn't socialism we're talking about—it's social democracy. I've decided the best way to clarify the point is simply to describe what social democracy Scandinavian style consists of. In Norway, 95 percent of the industry is privately owned. Only 3 percent of Norway is arable—yet they export farm produce. Scandinavian fish products are some the finest in the world. The Swede's make one of the world's best automobiles—Volvo. The Finns, because of the vast sparsely populated areas in the north, created cell phone technology in the early 1970s. Today, Nokia is still a leading innovator in this field. The list of highly competitive and productive Scandinavian companies is extensive. These are capitalistic countries—yet they understand that capitalism is inherently flawed. It doesn't serve every need or provide an answer to every question. Here is where the govenment steps in to accommadate the less fortunate, protect the environment from abuse, and provide affortable health care, among other things. Maybe it's like being out here in rough seas. You don't plow into it full throttle—but ease up and over those big seas.

MAY 17 : The water is clear, cold and blue. No heavy rains or big winds lately to make it dirty. I can see the top of my net, 24 feet down, easily. On the way in, I am going to swing by the old coal dock, just west of the mouth of Knife

River, and take a look at the wood cribbing beams on the bottom. I would like to get my hands on one of them.

The coal dock was part of the Alger Smith Railroad Line, completed in 1899, solely for the purpose of logging the old-growth white pine. In a mere twenty years they clear-cut the region of white pine. In 1919 the logging was finished. The last train ceased to operate in 1921 and by 1923 the tracks had been removed.

Most of the concrete laid on top of the timber cribbing has been demolished by the northeasters. There is one section of concrete, I could only guess it weighs 20 to 30 tons, that is in 25 feet of water 50 feet west of the original dock. That had to be a big sea to move it that far!

But my real interest in obtaining one of those old growth timbers on the bottom is for making musical instruments. The ring count on old growth white pine (softwood) is about 20 per inch. After they clear-cut, the wood that grows is what I would call "sun-drenched" and the ring count is only 4 to 12 per inch. The tighter the rings, the more resonant it is in musical instruments. There is another reason this wood is so valuable for instrument makers. Being underwater seems to change the structure of the wood, making it more resonant.

How I could ever get one of those big timbers out of the water is a major logistical challenge. But I'm thinking that the force behind one of the northeasters that causes my net anchors to drag might also loosen a timber down there someday.

MAY 28 : A sunny morning. Light wind out of the west. And the catch is just right for the day's orders—220 pounds. As I motor slowly into the west slip, I see that a couple of folks that want to buy herring "in the round" are waiting on the dock. If I don't have enough fish to fill the orders of the day, I can't sell fish in the round. But if I've got enough for my morning's restaurant, supermarket or smoke house order, I'll sell fish "right off the dock." This morning, Gary wants 50 pounds for smoking, fresh fillets and fishcake batter. Randy wants 20 pounds to fillet. He has some friends from Norway coming for a visit. The Norwegians should be delighted to have fresh herring.

As I see these two standing there, I'm reminded of another person waiting for fish, Clarence Swenson. Clarence lived on the shore, about halfway between Knife River and Duluth. Clarence probably started picking nets when he was old enough to row a boat. I know that he used the same fish house for 52 years. It was just across Scenic 61, right in front of his house. From the east end of Duluth almost to Knife River the land between Scenic 61 and the water's edge is Congdon Trust Land. It was given to the city of Duluth by the Congdon family with the agreement that it was never to be developed or used for commercial purposes. Clarence's fish house was on this property as were many others. A few years ago, a woman who'd recently moved here from the Twin Cities reported him to the authorities. The city of Duluth evicted him. Fifty-two years he had been there. The community knew Clarence was squatting—but what was the harm? They valued the tradition. Clarence was too old to fight back.

One evening he called me to see if he could buy some herring from me. He said he'd meet me at the dock. The next morning, when I motored up to the dock and saw him standing there, it broke my heart. He was reduced to buying herring for his supper from another fisherman.

Clarence died a few months later.

JUNE 3 : I have a visitor in my skiff this morning. An unwanted person. The president. I can't stop thinking about the terrible things George Bush has done to this country—and continues to do! I have two nets to lift yet and I don't think I can endure him anymore. I need to get him out of my skiff.

The light fog floats up and around allowing bits of sunrise to shine through. But inside my head it's a gale force wind. It's senseless to be out here in such a dark mood over this man's arrogance and incompetence. I could symbolically throw him overboard tied to that cement block I've got in the stern, but I'm too cheap to waste a good cement block on him. I *can* purge him from my skiff. I need to focus on the work I have to do, and on the beauty around me. Yes, lift the net up over the bow. And there, the flash of silver herring below in the clear, cold water. And now the sun peeks through the fog to warm my face.

JUNE 5 : It's a calm morning. Dave and his son just nudged their 14-foot boat close to me and I tossed them three herring. They're headed east of me about a half-mile. They'll drop an anchor down, shut off the motor and jig for lake trout using chunks of the herring for bait. I think they are fishing down about 140 feet. They have to use steel line to counter the current. They hardly burn any gas this way, unlike the trollers in their big boats. And they'll probably catch supper in a short time. It's sport fishing but with purpose.

Have you ever really thought about the word "sport" placed in front of fishing and hunting? Ultimately, it means "having fun" with an animal's life. Hunting and fishing are honorable and necessary. Most of the hunters and fisher-men I know love to be in the woods or out on the water. They respect and appreciate the food the animal provides. Why then is it called "sport"? In Alaska, residents are allowed to buy "subsistence" hunting and fishing licenses. The term sport might fit better alongside the egos of the trophy hunters and fishermen.

June 13 : The herring moved back in six days ago. Usually, when they come in, they'll stay for a while. June often is a stable month—the water is still cold and the hard currents don't tend to set in. The exception being if we get torrential rains and relentless hard northeast.

Harley Tofte fishes out of Grand Marais. He and his wife, Shele, own a seafood market called Dockside there.

Harley Tofte coming into Dockside in Grand Marais.

They sell a lot of herring at Dockside. Harley is probably one of the best fishermen on the North Shore. But like the rest of us, he goes through times when the herring just aren't around. He is in one of those "empty net" phases now. The fishermen up and down the shore try to help each other. He called on the 9th and said if I had any extra they could sure use it at Dockside. The next morning, I called as soon as I finished lifting. I had 265 pounds, in the round, I'd pack it in ice and they could have it all. We arranged to meet half way up the shore at Caribou River. On my way up, I picked up 60 pounds of fillets for Dockside from Walter Sve and Clint Maxwell. Walter and his son, Eric, fish near Split Rock, and Clint fishes out of Beaver Bay.

June usually is a good fishing month. But three days after I sold fish to Harley, the herring moved out, following their food supply. I only had eight pounds this morning.

Commercial fishing is sometimes compared to farming. Fishermen and farmers both have to deal with the vagaries of the weather. But farmers don't wake up one morning and see that their 80 acres of corn has moved to the next county.

JUNE 18 : As I look out my fish house door across to the woodshed, I can see two baby robins quietly sitting in their nest. It's the fourth year their mom has nested here. The first year I noticed her, she built a nest on the fluke of an anchor I had hanging on the east end of the woodshed. The next year, it was the back of the shed. The third year she put her nest in a balsam just to the west of my fish house. A blue jay devoured her eggs that year. And this year, the front of the woodshed.

How does she come to this small place every year?

Sanderlings, Red Knots, Whimbrels, Terns, travel thousands of miles and come to that one particular place.

And certainly the ability to find ones way over great distances isn't limited to the avian world. I remember reading about wolves that follow the migrating caribou in the Canadian Arctic. The wolves will make several kills, fill themselves and lay about for five or six days. When they get hungry again, they will travel in a straight line back to the caribou herd, which by then may have traveled a circuitous route a hundred miles farther north.

JUNE 21 : I grew up in a small town in northwest Wisconsin. It was a good place to grow up. For the most part, it was dairy farm country. Northeast of town though, was the terminal moraine (where the last glacier stopped) and the countryside was wooded with hills and lakes. Eight miles to the west of town, the Red Cedar River was slowly seeking its way to the Gulf. I knew creeks and fields and climbing trees in all directions from that small town. But deep down, even in those naive unformed kid cells and nerves, I knew it wasn't my place.

Just out of college, I camped on the beach east of the mouth of Knife River. When I crawled out of my tent the next morning and felt the northeast wind and watched the herring gulls soar and listened to the silence deep within the Lake, I knew, "This is where I belong." I still felt the urge to journey to other parts of the world, experience other things. But then one morning, as I headed to my nets, I was astonished to discover that the urge had vanished, the wanderlust had slipped from my consciousness. I said to myself, "I'm here!"

JULY 3 : I am in a womb of dark gray sea and sky this morning, picking the herring from the net; the rolling and twisting of my skiff, Herring gulls silently swimming around me.

But mostly I see my father climbing down a ladder to a Higgins Boat. None of the 36 men onboard speak as the diesel shudders the boat to the beach of Iwo Jima. And what comes to me again and again like waves thudding on the beach is his body, broken by Lou Gehrig's Disease, trying to lift itself off the floor yesterday morning, and me without words, lifting him to his feet.

JULY 26 : The heat of summer is here—not my favorite season. The Lake is calm. June's fog has lifted. On balmy, windless weekends, sport boats get as numerous as herring gulls on Knife Island. And, as often happens, just when the peak demand for herring fillets hits—when visitors are filling North Shore restaurants from Duluth to Grand Marias—the herring disappear.

I don't really know where they go. My first guess is that they disperse. My second guess is that they are "out and deep." Kenny and I always talked about setting a net "out" for July and August. But with his death, now it's a conversation of one. And there are problems with setting farther out in the lake. There are two shipping lanes I have to contend with. About once a week, an ore boat will come from Duluth to Two Harbors, hugging the shore. Hugging the shore in this case means about two and a half miles out. I set a net two miles straight out from Larsmont. I've been

picking herring off this net when ore boats pass bound for Two Harbors. They don't miss my outside buoy by more than a quarter mile.

The main shipping lane is five to six miles from shore at Knife River/Larsmont. That is right where a herring net should be set during the doldrums of July and August. Not a good idea. Even if the net was set 20 fathoms from the surface, I still need floats on the surface to adjust the depth of the net. If an ore boat or salty went over the net, I might get lucky. It could just cut all the lines supporting the net and it would just drop to the bottom. Then I would have to grapple it up from the bottom. Grappling a net up in 400 feet of water isn't so easy. A second problem is I'm not sure I want to run four miles straight out from shore for two months in a 18 foot skiff with only a foot and a half of freeboard.

So, summer after summer, when the herring disappear, sometimes in July, sometimes in August, I tough it out—

keep hoping for cooler, zooplankton-rich water to roll back in. And it does happen. It happened a few years ago in August. It was wonderful. In the middle of all the heat and humidity, dirty warm water down to 60 feet—one morning it was gone—clear, colder water with herring. What was even more gratifying, the herring were firm. When I do catch herring in warmer water, they are often so soft, it's hard to get good fillets out of them. They're fine if they're to be smoked. The brining toughens the flesh. They're not rotten; most of the fish are still living when I take them out of the net—just soft. And I won't sell them as fillets.

This morning, I've only managed to come up with 35 pounds of herring. Thirty-five pounds on 4 nets, totaling 1200 feet. The seas are calm and there's no hurry to get home. I'm taking the long way home—cruising the south side of Knife Island. The south side where mountain ash trees get the extra sun they need. There can't be much soil but it should be nutrient rich from all the gulls. As I approach the island, I'm delighted and surprised to see that the mountain ash berries have already turned red. This is a good sign.

JULY 29 : Orville Reese lived near Silver Creek, four miles northeast of Two Harbors. It was a good spot for skids, the bank was fairly flat. Like many of the other fishermen he would set his herring nets right out in front of his house. He could push his skiff off the skids and head to his herring nets only a quarter to a half-mile away. Orville also owned a fish tug. Tugs are too big to be pulled up on skids on a daily basis; he had to moor his in Agate Bay in Two Harbors.

Lifting the nets on a calm day.

The fishermen who owned tugs used them for lifting deep-water nets set for ciscoes. When the weather was nice, Orville would sometimes just anchor his tug out in front of his house instead of running to Two Harbors.

A northeaster started to build; Orville knew he needed to move his tug to Agate Bay. He called his helper, one of the Running boys. It was his 21st birthday. They pushed the skiff off the skids, motored to the tug, put the skiff in tow and headed to Two Harbors. The pilothouses on the old Lake Superior fish tugs were usually in the stern. This allowed for more space up front when lifting nets and it was easier to set the nets out the stern—one man could steer and slide the net while the other spread the net. These tugs were always fully enclosed for protection when lifting nets in November and December. They would have wood or coal stoves up front for warmth. When running to a net, up front was a nice place to sleep until you got to the net.

The northeast had built fast. They were just outside the break wall of Agate Bay when the pull of the skiff in tow ripped the stern out of the fish tug. Orville was suddenly in the water. He made it to shore. The Running boy was never found. The tug sank quickly—stern first. He probably was trapped in the bow as she sank.

AUGUST 18 : In the late 1980s, I sometimes worked on the passenger boats running to Isle Royale. Occasionally, I was privileged to work with Roy Oberg. Roy operated a number of vessels for Sivertson's for more than 30 years, hauling mail, groceries, fish and people to and from Grand

Portage and Isle Royale. Hiawatha, Disturbance, Voyageur I and Voyageur II. The Hiawatha had a pre-WWII Kahlenberg diesel engine. The engine looked like three large upside-down iron garbage cans. It had diesel fuel torches on each cylinder head that you needed to use to start it when it was cold. She was a slow boat.

Roy never bent a prop over those many years. But he came close one time running up Amygdaloid channel with the Hiawatha. He got a little too entranced in a Zane Grey book, looked up and he was headed straight to shore. He slammed the Hiawatha in reverse and steered for two big logs laying side-by-side perpendicular to shore. The Hiawatha nosed up on those logs, stopped, and slid gently unharmed back into the channel.

I remember him telling me that the weather changes on the Lake on August 18.

He's right.

August 19

The Fisherman's Wife

Just now
I saw her look down
at her hands on her lap
gently move that ring
back and forth a bit
like a boat softly rolling
on the sea

SEPTEMBER 10 : 6:30 AM. I'm out here. But it is difficult to tell you much of what is here. The lake, the sky, the wind. One of our Siberian Huskies died last night. Anna was a sweet girl. She asked very little. I can tell you little more…my spirit is in the depths of this vast dark water.

SEPTEMBER 16 : It's been blowing hard northeast the last two days. Even when I know I can't get out on the lake, I still come down and check my skiff. Yesterday morning, when I came down to make sure everything was ok, the gunwale of my skiff was flush with the dock. The water level always comes up with a strong northeast. But this time, it also must have combined with an extreme low-pressure system. Last night, the northeast let up. The wind then hooked around to the northwest 30 to 40 miles per hour. Northwest pushes the water directly away from the north shore. This northwest combined with high pressure, which pushes down on the water. This morning—my skiff is 18 inches lower! I've got a tape measure in my skiff. This is an accurate measurement.

A few years ago, I was working on my skiff at the dock. The wind was calm. I finished the job in the skiff and stepped onto the dock to mend a buoy. I had been standing there, working at least ten minutes, when I noticed that my skiff was flopping slightly—no wind, no other boat wake. I could see from the piers, the water had dropped three inches. The water moved out so quickly, it rocked my boat.

There is a word for this phenomenon: Seiche (saysh). I have never heard local folks or commercial fisherman use it. Rather than saying "there was a strong seiche today" people will say, "The water really came up with that northeast," or "Christ, did it drop after that northwest."

SEPTEMBER 20 : Their flight is quiet! I'm enjoying the low grey clouds scudding by as I slide along my net. Breaks in the clouds send bursts of sunshine on the shore far ahead—and warmth on my back. And suddenly, they are just off to my left—Pelicans! They glide just above the water. I didn't hear a sound. I watch them disappear to the south.

SEPTEMBER 23 : There's a bit of fog out here this morning. The North Shore comes into view, then disappears. Most puzzling, I can hear a songbird, or maybe two. I should be able to identify them just by their song. I'm worried about them. Songbirds shouldn't be out here. The yellow-rumped warblers are numerous now. I would guess they are what I'm hearing. I feel badly for them. They are stressed. This has been a dry summer and the insects are few. It is sad to see how many are killed by cars as they desperately seek food. They just arrived here from the boreal forest and tundra, innocent of the plague of speeding cars. They work close by my skiff—as if they know they are venturing too far from shore.

I finish picking the last net and head for the harbor.

The light fog and grayness give way to more light. Shades of blue appear in both sky and water. Near Stone Gate cabins, I see something flopping in the water. I steer towards it. It's a small songbird with waterlogged wings. It can't lift itself out of the water. I am able to gently cup it in my hand. It is a yellow-rumped warbler—exhausted and shivering. I keep it in my hand and tuck it inside my coat pocket the remaining ride home. I am surprised that a Herring gull, with its acute vision, didn't already eat this little songbird.

When I get to the marina, I put it in the front seat of my car. Even though it could dry off here, I'm still afraid the herring gulls would find it.  After I secure the boat and load the car, I find the shivering bird still sitting next to me as I start the car and head home. I turn the heat on high. I almost get delirious driving home—but it's what this little passenger needs.

At home, I park the car in the sunshine, open all the doors and start cleaning fish. About an hour later, I check the car to see if the traveler from the north is about. Not in the car—its search for food is in a little safer place.

SEPTEMBER 30 : Torg and his dad, Herb, met me at the dock this morning. Torg works full-time at the ore docks in Two Harbors. He has tended nets since he was a kid. His job keeps him from fishing most of the year, but when the fall herring run starts, he takes some vacation time. Herb has been "on the water" for many years. When he wasn't tending nets, he sailed on the ore boats. He fished his own rig on Isle Royale and the North Shore. Herb was typical of many North Shore fishermen, they often fished both Isle Royale and the North Shore. Isle Royale was and is a "lake trout factory." But most of the fishing families gave up after Isle Royale became a National Park. Some did opt for life-leases on their land and continued to fish until the death of the leaseholder.

When Torg was 16 years old, in 1972, he worked on an ore boat for the summer. The first down bound trip from Two Harbors was to Ohio. The ore boat unloaded its taconite at a facility in the mouth of the Cuyahoga River. One of the crewmembers mentored Torg. His mentor knew the river had started on fire in 1969. He wanted to show Torg what happened when you threw a rock into the river. Torg said, "It didn't splash. It just made a dull sploosh."

Three years had passed since the river started on fire. The Cuyahoga River was still heavily burdened with pollution in 1972. The Clean Water Act was enacted October 18, 1972. "Inherent flaws" started to be addressed.

I think Herb is 78 years old. It's great to see those two headed to and from their nets. Herb is the motorman. Their skiff pounds in a head sea. It's tough on the guy riding the bow. Torg has it figured out. He stands right behind the picking table and hangs on to the bowline. He can absorb the pounding much better with his legs than his back.

George Torgerson's gas boat "Rambler" with a typical Lake Superior herring skiff in front.

A picking table is simply a piece of plywood about 30 inches wide that sets flush with the gunwales and stretches across the skiff from one to the other. There are posts at the four corners to keep the net on the table as you slide along. Some fishermen use them, some don't. I'm not fond of them. I'm usually by myself and it's just another thing to crawl over to get to the bow.

Herb lost his father to Lake Superior when he was two years old. The fish tug "Hannah" has never been found. The four fishermen's bodies washed up on the beach.

George Torgerson's gas boat "Rambler" at Erickson Dock.

OCTOBER 12 : I don't need to put a thermometer in the water. No need to go on the Internet and check the surface temperature readings of Lake Superior. I can simply tell by the cold on my feet as I head to my nets—the lake has turned over.

OCTOBER 13 : Torg and Herb set their nets this morning. The fall herring run is about to begin.

I look forward to this time of year. I'll be damn tired by the end of it, but it's a good tired. If a fisherman can average about 600 pounds a day, that's perfect. I have to maintain my local fillet market and filleting is slow. Beyond that, my catch goes to a fish company called Interlaken. I "back split" the herring for them. You cut the head off and then slice the fish full length down the back. The fish then lays flat, belly up, and the roe can cleanly be separated. The roe is worth considerably more than the flesh. I can back split 70 pounds every 15 minutes.

The fish and roe are delivered to Grand Marais (Interlaken provides a truck to pick up the individual fishermen's catches). Shele' Tofte at Dockside oversees the processing of the roe into caviar. It's put into one-kilo tubs and blast frozen. Interlaken has been selling it to a company in Sweden. American's just don't know what they're missing out on. When I worked in Norway, I often had cod roe spread on a slice of buttered bread for breakfast or lunch. Roe (caviar), be it cod or herring, is an everyday food for the Scandinavians.

Approximately 90,000 pounds of the back split herring is salted. This is sold in Appalachia. It's an old English tradition.

By far the largest percentage of "back splits" is minced into gefilte fish. This is a Jewish fish cake or fish ball. The Canadian fishermen, the Minnesota fishermen northeast of Grand Marias, and Harley (who fishes out of Grand Marais) send their herring to the processing plant in Grand Marais "round." Obviously, they get less money for the fish this way, but they make up for it because they don't have to clean fish and are able to fish more volume. After the herring is back split, it's shipped to Stoller's Fisheries in Spirit Lake, Iowa, where it's minced for gefilte fish.

OCTOBER 16 : It's still dark as I turn my pickup into the west entrance of the marina. I shut my headlights off, then shut the engine off. Before I even open the door, I can hear it. I'm puzzled. It didn't blow hard northeast last night. I listen. Those are huge rollers crashing on the beach. I still can't figure out why I'm hearing these big slow breakers. Then I realize what happened—there must have been a strong north wind up the shore. A strong north wind makes those big slow swells.

Now I have to decide if I should head out in the dark. The fall herring run is on and to give myself every opportunity to get the herring picked off my nets before the wind starts blowing, I want to leave in the dark. I like to arrive at my first net with just enough light to find it. But if the weather is a little mean, with 3 to 5 footers, it's safer to wait until daylight. But the seas from a north wind are slow—they might be ten foot—but I'll just go up and over. I decide to head out. I can always turn around and come back into the marina if it doesn't feel good. I'm not going to be able to see much—I'll just have to feel them with my skiff.

I put on my rubber clothes, grab my flashlight and sandwich, head to my skiff. I make a second and third trip to get a dozen fish boxes out of the back of my truck. It is a clear night. Stars are still shining to the west. To the east, they're slightly dimmer. The city lights of Two Harbors, the ore dock lights and the lighthouse light are very clear. They provide me with a heading. I don't own a GPS. I don't bother with my compass unless there is fog. If I keep all the lights of Two Harbors on my port side just a little off the bow, I'll come up to my outside piece. I can also tell if I'm three miles east of the marina by aligning a bump in the Larsmont ridge and some yard lights on the shore.

Just past the break wall, I have to make a slow swing back towards the village of Knife River to run the gap between Knife Island and the mainland. My skiff isn't being rocked or bounced sharply—just an easy slow lifting up and down. This will be a fun ride. As I pass the rocks off the southwest end of the island, I steer northeasterly. I drop into a trough and see that the lights of Two Harbors disappear. Nothing too unusual about that. Let's see what happens to the red light on top of the tower on top of Pork City Hill. The next sea lifts me up then drops me down. The light disappears—this is going to be a fun ride!

OCTOBER 18 : There is a 40-mile per hour wind out of the northwest this morning. It feels like it might drop down later this afternoon and maybe I can lift my nets then. For now, it's a nice cool day, a good day to cut up some poplar that blew down at my neighbors. Except the neighbor lady came out and reprimanded me for wearing that nice sweater when I was working. I said there was "nothing better to wear in colder weather especially out on Lake Superior." And I explained to her that Georganne finds me great work sweaters and she loves wool as much as I do. Her great grandmother, who was blind at the time, taught her how to knit and she came from the Shetland Islands where they wear wool practically all the time and in Scandinavia and England too. Didn't matter, my explanations were futile, like trying to lift a net in a 50-mile per hour wind. Georganne should be here to defend me. Sweaters wear like iron and they shouldn't be put away in

Net/fish houses with Knife Island and old "coal dock" in the distance.

closets only for good occasions. Did you know that wives of the fishermen on the Shetland Islands and probably the Faeroe Islands knit patterns in the sweaters that indicated the fishermen were from that island? Georganne knit some of these patterns into a sweater for me, and if I wash up on the beach somewhere, they won't know which island I'm from because of the confusion of patterns.

Thank you for the wood. Bye.

OCTOBER 20: I have an apprentice. He started lifting nets with me three days ago. He won't be able to work with me every day, but at least he can get some time in this fall and early winter. Like me, he has no family ties to commercial fishing on the North Shore. In order to get my license, I also had to apprentice two years with someone who had a master license. In 1984, I started fishing with Sivertson's; Milford Johnson was the fisherman who apprenticed me. Sivertson's could only guarantee me one month's work—just for the smelt run. Sometimes, you simply need to move ahead with trust. I was with Sivertson's for more than 10 years, working with Milford up and down the shore from Duluth to Isle Royale.

When he's not fishing with me, my apprentice, Jason Bradley, will be managing a CSA farm with his wife, Cree. CSA stands for Community Supported Agriculture. In the spring of the year, the CSA members will buy shares of the produce that Jason and his wife will grow during the summer. As the harvest matures, Jason and Cree will divide the crop and deliver it to members on a weekly basis. This system provides up front money for Jason and Cree to plant in the springtime, and more importantly, provides members with locally grown organic vegetables and fruits throughout the summer and fall. Matters of diet and health aside, the members are likely to feel a little more connected to the earth and their community. Jason has told me that many of them are also excited about getting fresh herring!

OCTOBER 21 : Sometimes the trickiest (and probably most comical) walk or crawl I do is just trying to make it to the stern of my skiff after I've finished picking a net. The rubber pants, or bibs actually, fishermen wear don't help. They're bulky and as a friend once commented, "Your walk

has some waddle with those pants." Kids are more straight-forward: "You walk funny."

We just finished the third net and I think there are 15 boxes with seventy pounds of herring in each one. I think I'm gonna try and go over them. Maybe folks are right—I do need a bigger boat. Fortunately, there's not a big rolling sea. If there were, I would have unloaded after picking each net.

This last net we picked is only about a half mile from Torg and Herb's nets. They are still picking fish and there are plenty of herring gulls swirling around above them. Torg has had the best lifts this fall. It's funny how nets only a half-mile from one another can fish differently. Kenny used to fish in Sucker Bay, which is about three miles southwest of the Marina. I'd be fishing Larsmont three miles northeast of the Marina. Sometimes I'd do well and he wouldn't. And sometimes just the opposite. Then there are times when herring seem to be everywhere.

It will be a slow ride in.

OCTOBER 22 : Yesterday, after we finished loading my truck, we waited to make sure Torg and Herb got in safely. Their skiff was really plowing water. They had 18 boxes. After we loaded all their fish onto Torg's truck, Herb finished cleaning out the skiff, climbed onto the dock and said with a grin, "Jeeez, I thought we'd never get to the end of the net."

Tommy Eckel, who has fished out of Grand Marais his entire life, is in critical care at a hospital in Duluth. I

Fall herring run, Grand Marais

believe he is eighty years old. His family asked Harley to pull Tommy's skiff out of the water. They're concerned that if he gets home from the hospital, he'll try to set a net.

When people ask me why I commercial fish, I can't seem to find the words to explain it. But there is no need for words between me and Herb and Tommy and the rest.

OCTOBER 29 : There's a four-foot sea already. I've got 600 pounds of herring in my skiff and one net left to lift. I know there are another couple hundred pounds in that last net—and I just don't want to let it go. A voice in my head says: "I need the money." And another voice says: "Pushing too hard is what kills fisherman."

I drop the end of the net I've just finished, and do the keep-your-body-low shuffle to the stern so I'm not thrown out of the boat. I don't have much freeboard, maybe a foot and a half. It would be easy to end up overboard. The last net to lift is the closest to shore. It's about a quarter mile away. Before I head to it, I scan the open water to the northeast. It's not good. More white on the top of those waves. I knew that—just get to the last net and pick as fast as I can.

The northeast sea is off my starboard rear quarter. My skiff rides it fine. Still mostly four footers but a few five and six footers sweep under me as I steer to the inside piece.

As I start sliding along the net, I notice there is a little less northeast current pushing on this net. And because this is a newer net, not so ragged, it's easier—faster—to get the fish out. I say "thank you" and the wind carries my message. The first net I picked this morning is farthest from shore, about two miles. It's a rag—a lot of holes. Because of the stronger current out there and ragged net I probably spent an extra 15 minutes getting the herring out. Maybe I can scrounge enough money for a new net next year? Forget replacing this old outboard or buying an ice machine. One new net is probably it.

About two-thirds of the way through the net, the wind velocity has increased and the five and six footers have become more regular. My skiff rides just fine as I sit here picking the net. I remind myself of this when I think of the three-mile ride back to Knife River. Take it slow. The faster I push it, the greater the chance of losing control. I could easily start surfing on one of those six footers, broach or plow into the back of another wave and overwhelm the bow. Commercial fishing is patience, patience: waiting for a gale force wind to die down, waiting for the herring to move in, struggling to save enough money for a new net.

People say to me, "It's a pretty dangerous job, isn't it?" I find it odd what people come to accept as safe. It seems to me traveling down I-35 bumper-to-bumper with three-and-a-half ton SUVs at speeds of 75 to 85 miles per hour is insanity. How safe is one in an overpopulated world of people and machines? There are risks out here on the lake. The risk of being humbled. The risk of solitude. There is a Greenland Inuit saying: "It is not a good thing to steal another man's solitude." Out here, the cold and the wind won't let that happen.

NOVEMBER 4 : I knew there was going to be opposite current this morning. So did Torg, we checked in with each other before heading out. It's been blowing west for weeks with temps much colder than normal. The wind finally hooked around to the east last night. It's a moderate wind, but with the west current plowing right into it, the seas are steep. I just took one over the bow. I need to pull the floorboards out and take them home. It's easier to just let the heat of the woodstove in the fish house melt the ice than to try and pound it off. I probably have two hundred pounds of ice buildup.

The good thing is, the east might bring in more herring. I've had steady numbers—but not great—only 300 to 400 pounds a morning. I need to get some consistent 600 to 800 pound lifts. Our health insurance premium comes up in December.

NOVEMBER 7 : John is helping me lift nets this morning. He apprenticed with me four years ago. He has his own small aircraft repair business. In order to maintain your commercial fishing license, a fisherman has to work 30 days on the lake. John never intended to fish full-time. But the thirty days on the water is a nice diversion from his shop. Of the 25 commercial fishermen from Duluth to Grand Portage, about half are like me—full-time, and the rest have other primary jobs.

The wind is northeast and only intends on getting stronger. But John has good sea legs. Last year he was with me in a big sea from a north wind. I probably should not have lifted my nets that day. Torg tried, but turned around after a half mile of pounding. He watched us from the shore for a while, declared our insanity, and went off to do some other work.

There was one moment that morning I didn't like. We got up on the top of a big one and the skiff started to twist sideways. At the same time, the prop came out of the water and I couldn't steer. But then the prop was back in water, we dropped down into the next trough, the motor bogged down trying to climb up hill and we kept on going.

NOVEMBER 22 : The wind, the current, the overcast sky, the water temperature were perfect the last two days. They were perfect from Thunder Bay, Ontario, south to Knife River and back east to Cornucopia, Wisconsin. The processing plant in Grand Marais is overwhelmed. The processing plant in Spirit Lake, Iowa, is overwhelmed. I got the call from Tom Ophien at Interlaken—they can't take any more fish. The roe quality has dropped as well.

The same thing sometimes happened in Alaska when I fished sockeye salmon. Perfect conditions, usually at the peak of the run, and the canneries had to shut down the fishermen a few days. In this case, that's it for the fall herring run and selling fish to Interlaken. I'll tie 'em up. After Thanksgiving, I'll run out and drop a net or two. The local market is always good in December.

DECEMBER 2 : The marina is ice-covered right to the end of the east breakwall. I jump down into my skiff—it doesn't move. I stand up on a gunwale and jump—still doesn't move. I start busting ice with an old oar. A couple of whacks and I break through. It's about an inch and a half thick. The first thing to do is break around the outboard and get it started. As I do this, I remind myself to pull gently on the recoil the first time. An outboard gets a little stiff at 9 degrees Fahrenheit. You want to make sure to loosen things up before pulling hard. Otherwise, the recoil rope or my shoulder might shred.

After I crack some more ice in front of the bow, to give myself a little running room at the ice, I give it a try. My flat-bottomed steel skiff works well for breaking ice. I make a circle away from the dock and come back to my original spot. I head out to the end of the ice at the outer breakwall and swing back to run through it again. I need to get this ice busted up so the northwest wind can carry it out. I need to get out to my nets before the wind gets much stronger.

The frost smoke is heavy out on the lake. Impish ice spirits dancing everywhere.

DECEMBER 4 : Eric Sve called. He was wondering if I was still catching fish at four fathoms? It was a good thing he called. I wasn't paying attention. I could see the herring were dropping off. As the water gets colder, we usually lower our nets. I started by just lowering one net to six fathoms. My catch went from 20 pounds to 140 pounds. Needless to say, I lowered the other nets to six fathoms too. A good lesson for the master license and my apprentice is doing quite well, thank you! He was wondering why, as many people do, we measure things in fathoms. The arm spread of the average person is about 6 foot—one fathom. I can use 2500 feet of line (rope) for just one net. It is a fast and functional way to measure out significant amounts of line. That 2500 feet of line is for a net in 400 feet of water, which is about the deepest I have out of Knife River. Clint Maxwell has 800 feet of water to deal with out of Beaver Bay.

DECEMBER 5 : Five below zero last night. The stars shone brightly and the wind slept. A perfect night to make ice—an inch and a half thick the full length of the marina. Same routine—break the ice around the outboard, get it started, break the ice around the rest of my skiff until I can

Spring storm, 1937, at Severin Martinson and Nels Lind's dock.

rock it freely. And have faith in the long-range forecast—that it will warm up in a few days.

The wind might have rested during the night, but as soon as daybreak hit, it started in out of the west. West wind—if my motor breaks down, I'm quickly bound for the middle of the lake and then on to the Apostle Islands or Canada. By then, I might be a frozen lump. When I listened to some of the old-timers talk, it became clear that most of the deaths on the North Shore occurred before gas engines. A strong northwest or west would hit. Unable to row against it, they would quickly find themselves miles from shore. Their only option then was to put out a sea anchor, keep bailing water and try to keep from freezing. Some were never found. Some were found frozen to death on the South Shore. One of the lucky ones, Magnus Martin was rescued. When they got him ashore, they had to use an ice chisel to chip his boots out of the bottom of his skiff.

This morning, the frost smoke is as thick as June fog. But I'll find my nets—I need to get them lifted before this wind gets any stronger.

DECEMBER 6 : The main channel of the marina is wide open! What a relief! The weather forecast was wrong. I woke up this morning expecting to pound ice again. It was fifteen degrees below normal last night but the wind was out of the north. And that creates a northeast sea, which has pushed warmer water into the marina. I can see that it's slightly discolored from the turbulence. Not only that, the water level came up three to four inches further, helping to

bust up the ice. I've got some breathing room for a couple of days—maybe.

There are three- to four-foot steel gray seas on my beam as I head to the net. A nice change from the relentless west and northwest these past five days. They aren't sharp—the wind isn't pulling the tops off them—I'm not getting any spray in the face. Christ, yesterday coming in with that strong west wind I was plastered with spray. When I got inside the marina and stood up, the ice falling off me sounded like plate glass shattering. My face and beard were a little bit stiff. Today, I have a view. Steel gray sky, steel gray seas. Quite lovely!

Ice. The reality for those who harvest from waters in the Northern Latitudes. In springtime, New Foundlanders take boats up Davis Strait to the ice edge and send men out on the ice floes to harvest seals. On Great Slave Lake, in the interior of Canada, commercial fishermen can't get their boats out until the spring breakup which usually occurs in late July. The crab fishery in the North Pacific is a winter fishery. If the crew isn't hauling in 500 pound crab pots in fifteen-foot seas, they often have to take hammers to bust off the ice that has accumulated on the superstructure. Ice buildup can easily make a boat dangerously top heavy. The last summer I fished Sockeye Salmon in Alaska was 1998. I was 45 years old. At the end of the season, in the boatyard, I met some folks who owned a crabber. I always wanted to try it. I asked them if they needed crew. The owner shuffled his feet a bit and looked down at the ground. Finally, he said, "I don't mean to insult you, but you're too old."

DECEMBER 7 : Outboard trouble this morning. Luckily, I have Jason to help me. We pulled the 25 horse Yamaha off; I have a feeling the impeller spun off the key-way on the shaft. I have an extra impeller, but I'll fix it later at home. For now, the quick fix was to grab Squeak's 9.9 just a few blocks away. Not much power, and the gas line I got from him is bad, the squeeze-ball was rock hard so Jason switched that from another line I had and then we switched the connector to the tank 'cause I have a confusion of gas tanks i.e. Mercury, Yamaha, OMC. But not to worry, we're cruising home, though I have to keep squeezing the squeeze-ball—otherwise the motor quits. We're headed in the right direction, and to paraphrase badly an Old Norse saying, "There is no point going out your door fearful in the morning because the time of your death has long since been appointed." The only problem is, I swear I read that in a friend's book but then I went back and couldn't find it, and then I told my good friend Louis Jenkins, the poet, about it and he looked through all the Old Norse texts and couldn't find it and then he said, "Are you sure you read that?" and I said, "Sort of." Then he said, " Maybe you thought it up?" And then I said, "I don't think so. But things do get blurry."

And so Jason is wondering why he keeps bringing a thermos cup of coffee with him when we go out on the lake. When he finally gets around to it, it's frozen solid or went flying around the bottom of the skiff when we rolled or pounded and is full of herring scales and slime. We're headed in and we caught 320 pounds which makes me very happy and we had, as usual, very good conversations, and yes the critical problem is overpopulation and no one addresses it and now Jason is thinking about how to solve the coffee crisis. I think a propane torch would solve the freezing coffee problem.

DECEMBER 9 : Smoke is curling up and around from the back of Kendall's. I know that Gordy and his son, Cody, are filling racks with herring, ciscoes, lake trout and salmon to slide into the smoker.

There was a very light wind at home; I thought I'd get out. But it's blowing 20 to 30 miles an hour on the lake. It's one of those mornings Squeak describes best—"The lake is making its own weather." Squeak sometimes would add an expletive to his description. It gets frustrating when you

can't get out there... you just go home and find something else to do, and there is always plenty to do. Boredom can be struck from my vocabulary. There are things to finish on the house. But I like the Chinese proverb, "Man finish house, man die." Obviously not meant to be taken literally, but I like to exploit it that way.

Even at Kendall's, which is only a quarter-mile away from the beach, you can't tell how hard it is blowing out there. I've stopped in here before, and Gordy says, "How much fish do you have for us this morning?" I shake my head and say, "It would be suicide to go out there."

The smoker is in a building attached to another building. Off to the east is the freezer; it kind of sits at an angle. Beside it are two old truck trailers. Gordy Olson and Kristi Olson-Kendall are taking over the business from Kristi's dad, Russ Kendall.

I can see the glow of the maple fires as I walk into the backroom. They leave the big smoker doors cracked open to get the fires going before they slide the racks in. Gordy asks, "How much longer are you going to fish?" I say, "I'm trying to hang in there until the 21st or so. How much more herring do you need to get through until next April?" Gordy stops hooking ciscoes and ponders the question. There are tubs of brined fish against the wall. Cody is sprinkling brown sugar on chunks of lake trout. He says, "We better get more fillets for fishcake batter. We ran out last year." Gordy nods his head and says, "We should get at least 40 more pounds of fillets and 200 pounds of smokers."

"OK, I'll let you get back to work."

And the nice thing is, if I show up tomorrow with half the order, that will be fine. And if I show next Tuesday with the full order, that will be fine too.

Jason picking herring.
The net freezes instantly.

DECEMBER 10 : There is water coming into my skiff. I know the bottom is still solid, but all it takes is one little pinhole. Crunching through ice doesn't help. I've suspected for the last couple of days that it was leaking. Before I headed out this morning, I found the hole up in the bow. It's still leaking, I'll take care of it when I get in. I carry a piece of dowel with me in the skiff. I can always cut a plug if too much water comes in.

When I fished for Sivertson's, I had to fit a wooden plug in the bottom of a steel pond net boat. We used the boat with the plug in it for the rest of the smelt season.

In 1927, on Isle Royale, the operator of a tug who was rushing to help the America, which had just sunk in North Gap, knocked a hole in his boat. A crewmember grabbed the mattress from his bunk and stuffed it in the hole. They took the tug all the way back to Duluth with that "mattress plug."

Actually, my biggest concern is that I need more fish. The phone keeps ringing. "I need a hundred pounds of dressed." "We need 50 pounds of skinless fillets." "We need more herring for fish cake batter." It's hard to convince some folks that that the weather is a little bit nasty or that sometimes the herring simply aren't around. In early November of this year, Torg told me he got a call for 10 pounds of fillets. He told the woman he couldn't get out on the lake because of the weather. She got angry and hung up. Torg shook his head and said, "It was blowing 40 miles an hour out of the Northeast. You'd think she could make a connection." But these are good problems.

I've finished picking my nets and am headed in. I'm thankful for another morning on the lake. To the east is Knife Island. I can see a bald eagle perched on a scraggly dead balsam. The island belongs to him during the fall and into winter. There are a handful of herring gulls sitting on the end of the west breakwall. They remain motionless as I go by. I pass near enough to the breakwall that I can smell the creosote in the timber. Ahead, at the end of the dock, someone is standing. It's Erickson. He doesn't want fish this morning. He checks on me regularly. I shut the outboard off and drift to the dock. He says, "How much longer are you gonna keep fishin'?" A gust of wind twirls snow in front of him. He pulls his hat down a little more snugly and says, "I worry about you out there by yourself."

"I have a different problem," I say. "I've got a hole in my skiff."

I can see he's thinking about this. "I have some marine epoxy at home. It will set up under water. I don't know how it will work in this cold? You wanna try it?"

"Ya."

"I'll go get it. I'll be back in 10 minutes."

DECEMBER 16 : The graffiti on the underpass wall of the railroad bridge coming into Knife River tells me "The world is ending as we know it." I love the play in this—the twist on the doomsday scenario. My world will certainly be "ending as I know it" in a week or so when I pull my nets for the season. But mostly it will be the same. Getting up before sunrise, starting a fire in the woodstove, making some coffee.... One of the things I love about our huskies (dogs in general) is they are amazingly aware of the world around them. They'll know the morning is different minutes

after I get up. They'll know the winter routine is about to begin. I don't head to the lake right away; instead we walk to meet the rising sun.

Squeak and Kenny used to have a 35-foot fish tug, the Nels J. She was wood with steel plating on the hull. Squeak used to break ice in the marina with her. But even with the steel plating, he said she'd leak a bit for a few days after he broke up the ice. Mel Bugge owned the Nels J. back in the 50s. When the ice was too heavy, Mel would just use dynamite to loosen it up. My world would certainly "end as I know it" if I tried that.

DECEMBER 21 : The last net is pulled out of the water and into the skiff. Jason and I are headed in. Buoys, fish boxes, floats, line are piled from bow to stern. Jason is trying

to straighten it out. "Enjoy the ride home. I've got all winter to sort this mess out. We'll just throw it all in the back of the truck." He kerplunks down on the seat in the bow.

This is the beginning of my time of rest. It occurs to me that it's the solstice. The ancient agrarians of Europe celebrated on this day. They were a culture that transformed from hunter/gatherers to sowers of seeds. They honored the return of light—the lengthening of the days—and the ability to grow food again. While I'm thoroughly enmeshed in the modern world, I find comfort living and working with the cycles of the earth.

I'm saddened how few people understand the intertwining of the present holidays with these ancient traditions. How few ponder the origin and meaning of the Christmas tree. For many cultures, a piece of greenery in the home symbolized eternal life at a dark time of the year. (It also explains why cemeteries are often surrounded by yew or cedar trees.) How few people reflect, during Easter, on the presence of those very non-Christian symbols of the "egg" and the rabbit as symbols of fertility. For seeds to grow and domestic animals to reproduce, fertility needed to be honored.

As we make this last trip in for the season, I need to honor full boxes of herring, empty boxes of herring, steel gray seas and clouds, blue skies, northeasters—another season on the lake.

Knife Island is just off to the southeast. An eagle lifts off a dead fir. I'm just about to tell Jason to throw it a couple of herring. But thoughts are harmonized; he is kneeling at the box of fish. He grabs a herring and tosses it in the water. He grabs another and tosses it too.

We both watch aft as I continue on towards the marina

entrance. The eagle circles, swirls down, then circles up again. He circles a second time closer to the water. Another circle, lower, legs extend, a silver fish rises to the sky.

I turn around and nod to Jason. Home we go.

Epilogue

April 12 : I'm sitting in the swing that hangs on the front of my woodshed. The April sun is warm on my face. The huskies are enjoying it too—lying on a bed of sawdust where I cut firewood this winter. Overhead, a raven croaks. Across my work yard is my fish house. Nets have been pulled over and are ready to set. Anchor line has been boxed. Floats with six fathoms of line wrapped around them ready to be tied on the nets.

Flag buoys are propped against a stack of firewood. The flags pop and snap with a gust of wind.

About the Author: Stephen Dahl's earlier years include work in North Norway, a year of study in Denmark and graduate work in Scandinavian literature and languages at the University of Minnesota. He has commercial fished in Alaska and, for the last 24 years, the North Shore of Lake Superior. He resides with his wife, Georganne, and two Siberian huskies, near the village of Knife River.